Vladimir Antonov

Sathya Sai Baba —

the Christ of Our Days

Translated from Russian
by Anton Teplyy and
Mikhail Nikolenko

2008

ISBN 978-1438252766

Published in 2008 by CreateSpace

This book was created at the request of Sathya Sai Baba. Published in Russian, it was blessed by Him in His Indian ashram. Later the text of the book was supplemented with conversations with Him.

www.sathya-sai-baba.org

Contents

The Advent of Sathya Sai Baba

He was born in 1926 and named Sathya Narayana Raju.

In childhood, He was liked by everyone, because He was always kind, forgiving all offences from playmates, never "requiting evil with evil". And more... in school, He entertained other pupils by giving them sweets, which He took out from an apparently empty bag, materializing them.

At the age of 14, He told to His parents that He would not go to school any more, because He knows everything. And that He is a reincarnation of well-known in India Muslim saint Sai Baba (*Baba* means Father in Sanskrit) from the place called Shirdi. And that He wants to leave parents' home in order to dedicate His life to helping people, preaching the Truth about God, and about the Way of attainment of the Highest Freedom in Mergence with Him.

His years of childhood and adolescence are described in detail in a remarkable book of Samuel Sandweiss [4]; everyone interested can find this information there. I only want to notice, in order to help you understand the content of this book better, that Sathya Sai Baba, living in the shaivistic partly-pagan environment, did not oppose it. On the contrary, He supported people's faith by materializing, for example, attributes of the shaivistic symbolism.

Later on He explained it thus: "Each man begins cognition of the world through its forms. People cannot at once picture to themselves God as the Omnipresent Who is present in each object and in each individual. ... (Therefore), idols are necessary in order to point to God. To those, who have not realized God, idols are necessary. After the realization of God, idols become unnecessary. ... Worshiping an idol and acquiring through such worship experience of Divinity, one will be able to describe to oneself the feeling of God." [5]

All preaching activity of Sathya Sai Baba is accompanied by His demonstration of miracles.

He did this even in school years: He materialized sweets, pencils, rulers, and so on, and also won easily in running among other pupils by transporting instantly His body from the start to the finish.

In the following years, He converted adult atheists to believers, for example, by materializing in front of them, sitting at the table, the dishes which were "ordered" mentally by each one of them.

And now, materialization of various objects is a part of everyday activity of Sathya Sai Baba, by which He helps people to strengthen their religiousness.

As the preaching activity of Sathya Sai Baba developed, a group of faithful followers gathered around Him; an ashram was built, in which pilgrims could stay. Financial support from interested people made it possible to create in India a system of medical and educational institutions supervised by Sathya Sai Baba and to begin publishing books. Thanks to books and films, the name of Sathya Sai Baba is well-known now on all continents; He has millions of followers.

He brings to people salvation from the darkness of atheistic ignorance and religious misunderstanding. Let us — as souls — approach Him!

Who Is Sathya Sai Baba

His body is of medium height; His skin is dark as typical of all Indians; He wears orange monastic robes. A particular feature of His appearance is a shock of bushy, dark, curly hair.

But this is just His body, just a tiny part of Sathya Sai Baba...

In reality, He is completely different. He is the Oceanic Universal Consciousness connected with the material body. And in any part of the planet where it is necessary, It appears as a tongue of non-material Divine Flame, which rises above the surface of the Earth for kilometers[1]. The tongues of this Flame emerge in every place, where He is helping His disciples. It is enough just to call Him.

Yes, this is It — the Divine Fire, Which makes sinners tremble with fear, but does not have the quality of heat for righteous men, Which is the Subtlest of the subtle, Which is Tenderness, Bliss, Divine Love for all who became like It and entered It! Or It enters them and fills them with the Love of God.

Souls, which He touches in such a way, can hear His precepts, instructions, pieces of advice. They can do it if they, as consciousnesses, are pure and subtle enough, if they are capable of attuning themselves to the perception of Him forgetting about the problems of the material plane.

"There are 3 stages of concentration," Sathya Sai Baba says. "At the first stage, you receive My messages in the form of mental waves. At the second stage, you can hear My voice. And at the third, you can hear Me and also see. If you succeed in the purification of the consciousnesses, you will move from stage to stage.

---

[1] About Divine Fire see the book *Agni Yoga* by Vladimir Antonov.

"... When the mind is motionless and silent, one can hear the voice of God. Anyone who was able to purify the mind from anxiety, agitations, and thoughts can attune oneself to the voice of God inside." [12]

... Sometimes He takes on another appearance — more condensed, of just several meters in height. In this case, even people who have not purified themselves as consciousnesses to the necessary level are able to see Him.

But always — in any appearance — He can be recognized by His constant distinctive feature: a magnificent head of hair!

And let nobody think that while He is communicating, for example, with the author of this book, the rest of His disciples are left without His attention and supervision. No: in each moment, from His Abode come as many tongues of His Fire as necessary for satisfying the needs of all! Because He is an integral Part of the Primordial Universal Consciousness and His Power is unlimited!

He speaks about Himself in such a way: "I am the Sai Baba of Shirdi come again; then, I was mostly engaged in preparing the meal; now I have come to feed you all with the strengthening, purifying repast!" [8]

"I came to restore the Straight Path to God!" [1]

His Teachings

He does not say that His Teachings are new. His Teachings are just one more manifestation, for the contemporary conditions on the Earth, of the Divine Teachings, which God constantly repeats through His Messengers. These Teachings are called in Sanskrit *Sanathana Dharma* — the Eternal Law. "Sanathana Dharma is the mother of all religions, all ethical codes, and all laws of the universe," says Sathya Sai Baba [7].

He — Sathya Sai Baba — is the Avatar of our days. He says that though all conceivable powers of the universe are contained in His Palm, He is not going to make happy everyone without distinction, because each man has his personal destiny (karma), which he created by his good or bad past thoughts and deeds. By our present deeds we create our future destinies.

In order to escape from the abyss of earthly suffering, it is necessary to live in love for God and all living beings, including creative love-service to other people. The service to people, which consists in helping them in their positive evolution, is service to God.

The main enemies of man, leading to accumulation of negative karma, are the wrongly directed mind and uncontrollable emotional sphere with dominating egotistical or coarse emotions.

Man can overcome these obstacles by strengthening faith, by directing the mind toward the Divinity, and also with the help of spiritual practices, which, first of all, normalize the emotional sphere and help to learn how to control the mind and consciousness.

But the mind, as such, is not an enemy of man at all. On the contrary, it is an embryo of wisdom (jnana) and should be developed in every possible way as an analyzing and creative function of the consciousness.

In order to clean one's path from the karmic impediments, it is important to repent all small or big crimes committed against any living being. "By sincere repentance all sins can be washed. God's Mercy is responsive. If He has a wish to forgive, nothing can prevent this... In spite of past sins, if there is deep remorse and love for God, then all sins get washed, and the nature of man becomes clean. To be afraid that this will not happen is weakness. God has unlimited compassion; look for His love and you will find forgiveness!" [2]

"The most important spiritual practice is the search of one's own imperfections and weaknesses, and making attempts on ridding oneself of them, becoming closer to the Perfection" [6].

For strengthening the orientation of the mind toward God, Sathya Sai Baba recommends using the technique of frequent repetition of God's name and participating in divine worships with singing praise to God.

Gaining of faith is the first step. The next step in this direction is love for God. But how can people fall in love with the One Whom they do not know yet? This is why Divine Teachers come to the Earth to help people; the Unmanifest reveals Itself in the manifested for people form. Love for the manifested, personified aspect of God is more convenient for incarnate people.

But people should also understand that Sathya Sai Baba is not only in His body: He is everywhere, wherever He is needed. Therefore, it is not necessary to go to His ashram in order to talk with Him; it is possible to talk with Him right from your home.[2]

All people have only one God, Sathya Sai Baba teaches. And they must not divide themselves because of the variations of their beliefs. Let everyone worship One Universal God using their traditional variations of worship.

---

[2] But this requires that the main part of the work on cleansing and refinement of consciousness be done. Otherwise, you, being in coarse eons, will hear the voices of their inhabitants — demons, devils, probably mistaking these voices for the voice of God Who is yet too distant and unknown to you.

What really divides people is not the variations of faith, but the levels of the spiritual culture. Imagine for example, says Sathya Sai Baba addressing male students of a college, that according to the principle of equality of all people you marry a Muslim girl, who is used to eating meat. What will happen? Conflicts and discord?

But Sathya Sai Baba does not want that people be at enmity with each other because of differences in nutrition: let secular people eat meat. But if you walk the spiritual Path, then *the ethical aspect of nutrition has to be observed impeccably!* [2]

It is not possible to come to God without possessing perfect love, because He Himself is Love and lets in only those similar to Him. And the main principle of Love is compassion for all living beings — from plants and animals — to Divine Messengers.[3]

Concerning using fish for food, Sathya Sai Baba notes that these animals also die in suffering.

Once Sathya Sai Baba sent a group of His disciples to monastic seclusion in the mountains.

---

[3] The same was taught by Jesus Christ. But people did not include His words about this in the New Testament.

The purpose of this seclusion was meditative training. And in order that disciples did not distract themselves from this training by seeking food, He gave them a jug in which, every day, they could find enough food materialized by Him. What was in their "menu"? Rice, vegetables, beans, fruit, juices, and before night (before going to bed) everyone had a glass of milk. [1]

Killing-free nutrition is favorable for purifying the mind and consciousness. If one gets up early and goes to bed early, it also helps to clean the mind and consciousness. The second thing that a neophyte in religion should do is to refuse to concentrate the mind on negative traits of other people. Each person is potentially God. See God in everyone. Love everyone as the manifestation of God for you. I teach you by using the negative and positive traits of other people.

People differ by the qualities of the personal "ego", the "i".

In particular, there are deeply fallen, degraded souls, who like to do evil. They can do evil even without any reward. This is their nature: they are like a moth that gnaws and tears things no matter what they are; it equally gnaws a rag and an expensive sari [8].

But even such people are used by God in the general process of the Evolution of consciousness. From their example, other people can learn not to be like them and thus can know both good and evil. And they will be able, by pushing themselves away from evil, to go the path of good, toward the Perfection, toward the Mergence with God. One should know both: what kind of person one must not be and what kind of person one must be. It will be difficult to know good if one does not know evil.

Evil people are used by God also for correction of the development of true sadhakas (spiritual warriors). In particular, in this way God reminds sadhakas about coming death, and this allows them not to relax excessively on the Path.

Death and God are the most important landmarks for all incarnate people, says Sathya Sai Baba.

Evil people doom themselves to hell and suffering in the next incarnations. However, they, too, are given a chance for salvation: to reform and repent. Repentance is conscious remorse that leads to liberation from the vices.

Concerning the ethical self-correction, Sathya Sai Baba says the following [8]:

Those who seek the bliss in the Atman should not run after the joys of sense objects.

Just as a body that has no breath is useless and begins to rot and stink, similarly, life without the

Truth is useless and becomes the stinking abode of strife and grief.

Believe that there is nothing greater than the Truth, nothing more precious, nothing sweeter, and nothing more lasting!

The Lord who is Sathya grants His darshan (the possibility to contemplate Him) to those of truthful speech and loving heart.

Keep undiminished kindness toward all beings and also the spirit of self-sacrifice.

You must also possess control over the indriyas, an unruffled character and non-attachment.

Be always watchful against the following sins: 1) speaking falsehood, 2) speaking ill of others, 3) backbiting, 4) talking too much. 5) killing, 6) adultery, 7) theft, 8) drinking intoxicants 9) the eating of flesh. 10) sexual cravings 11) anger, 12) greed, 13) "earthly" attachments, 14) impatience, 15) hatred, 16) egoism, 17) pride.

First give up the evil tendency to feel envious at the prosperity of others and the desire to harm them. Be happy that others are happy! Sympathize with those who are in adversity and wish for their prosperity. That is the means of cultivating love for God.

Patience is the strength which man needs!

Those anxious to live in joy must always be doing good!

One should never give reply in swear words. Be at a great distance from them; this is for your good. Break off all relations with people who use such words!

Seek the company of good men, even at the sacrifice of your position and life. But be praying to God to bless you with the discrimination needed to distinguish between the good men and the bad. For this, you must endeavor with the intellect given to you.

Those who conquer states and earn earthly fame are hailed as heroes; but only those who have conquered the indriyas are heroes who must be acclaimed as the conquerors of the universe.

Whatever acts, good or bad, man may do, the fruits of them follow him and will never stop pursuing him.

Greed yields only sorrow; contentment is best. There is no happiness greater than contentment!

The tendency to make harm should be plucked out by the roots! If allowed to exist, it will undermine life itself!

Bear with fortitude both loss and grief! Try to achieve joy and gain in the future!

From this moment, avoid all bad habits! Do not delay, do not postpone businesses for the future: it will not contribute the slightest benefit.

Try as far as possible within your means to satisfy the needs of the poor, who really live in poverty. Share with them whatever food you have and make them happy at least that moment.

Whatever you feel should not be done to you by others, avoid doing such things to others.

For faults and sins committed in ignorance, repent sincerely; try not to repeat the faults and sins again! Pray to God to bless you with the strength and the courage needed to stick to the right path!

Do not allow anything to come near you, which will destroy your eagerness and enthusiasm for God. Lack of eagerness will cause the decay of the strength of man.

Yield not to cowardice! Do not give up bliss!

Do not swell with pride when people praise you! Do not feel dejected when people blame you!

If among your friends one hates another and starts a quarrel, do not attempt to inflame them more and make them hate each other more! On the contrary, try with love and sympathy to restore their former friendship.

Instead of searching for others' faults, search for your own faults! Uproot them, throw them off! It is better to find one fault of yours than to find tens of hundreds of faults in others!

If you cannot or will not do any good deed, then at least do not conceive and carry out any bad deed.

Whatever people may say about your faults that you know are not in you, do not get upset! As for the faults that are in you, you must try to correct them yourself, before others point them out to you.

Do not harbor anger or bitterness against persons who point out your faults; do not retort, pointing out the faults of those persons themselves, but show your gratitude to them.

Trying to point out to people their faults is a great mistake!

It is good if you know your faults; it is bad if you search faults in others.

Whenever you get a little leisure, do not spend it in talking about all and sundry, but utilize it in meditating on God or in doing service to others.

Only the bhakta (the one who loves God) understands the Lord; only the Lord understands the bhakta. Others cannot understand them. So, do not discuss matters relating to the Lord with those who are not bhaktas.

If anyone speaks to you on any subject, having understood it wrongly, do not think of his wrong opinions, but grasp only the good and the sweet in what he says.

If your worldly desires do not get fulfilled, do not blame it on the love of God: there is no relationship between such desires and the love of God!

If your meditation does not progress properly, do not get dispirited! When such feelings come, seek for your flaws!

It is only when in your daily conduct you behave automatically according to these rules, that you can perceive the Divine principle very easily! Therefore, hold on to these maxims firmly!

However, Sathya Sai Baba notes that all ethical teachings can be expressed in one short formula of Vyasa: "Help[4] ever, hurt never!".

The ultimate task of each man consists in cognition of the Higher Self, which is the Atman, Paramatman, the Creator. But for this purpose, the lower self, which manifests itself as egocentrism and which is created by the mind, must be eliminated.

The mind in this context is a part of the consciousness captured by "earthly" *desires*.

Desires are not thoughts. Thoughts become *desires* when they "submerge" deeply into objects.

---

[4] Help everyone in everything good!

Desires directed toward worldly objects cause pleasure and suffering. But if a desire is directed toward God, then it gives bliss! [2]

The ability to think correctly has to be developed through the "earthly" affairs. Then it can be transformed into a function of the buddhi. For this purpose, the "tentacles" of the consciousness (indriyas) should be redirected from the objects of the material world, even the best ones, toward the Divine Consciousness. The thinking of such progressively developing people in all their affairs rises to a fundamentally different level, because at this stage they, step by step, begin to learn to see the "earthly" problem as God sees them. The egocentrism of such a person gets gradually substituted with Godcentrism.

How can one get rid of the vicious work of the mind, which impedes further advancement? — Very simply: do not try to "muffle" it, but just think about God! The nature of the mind is such that it is necessary for it to be preoccupied with something, so let it be preoccupied with God! And when it is preoccupied with God, it stops. [2]

If you are not able yet to do this, then occupy it with repetition of the name of God or with another useful activity.

The uncontrolled mind is like a snake. It has two tendencies: it moves not straight and captures all things which it sees. But it should be forced to move straight to God, turned directly toward Him.

When the thinking of progressing man is performed not by the mind, but by the buddhi, then the buddhi submerges into God in order to become Him.

This is why it is so important to accustom oneself to being turned by the face (of the consciousness) toward God. [2]

There are two main themes that one should always member about: the coming death and God. And there are two main themes that one should forget: the evil caused by others to you and the good done by you to others. "Of course, it is essential to remember about the death, because this helps one to do many good things and avoid doing many bad things" [2].

"Time is the most precious gift in this world. Do not waste it saying ill words or doing bad deeds! ... One must not waste time! It will not wait for anyone. ... It is impossible to return the moment which has been wasted; it is lost forever... Nobody knows when death comes. The hand of time can crush you at any moment...

"In your deeds you should rise to the level of heroes and be not weak-willed people!

"Remembering about one's own death leads to 'unidirectional resoluteness'" [7].

"Before death, the position, pride, and power, all vanish. Realizing this, strive day and night, with purity of body and mind and spirit, to realize the Higher Self, by the serving all living beings.

"The body should be supported and kept as an instrument for this purpose.

"But remember, you are not these bodies, and these bodies are not you." [7]

"This body is but an instrument, a tool given by the Lord. And let it serve its purpose" [7].

One should take care of the body: it is an instrument for development of oneself, for one's God-realization. It should be washed, fed, healed if it falls sick; at that, there are no any contraindications for using medicaments and other medical means. [2,7]

But food is not a means for getting pleasure! Food is like fuel for a car. It is an essential element in service to God.

Remembering about the approaching death should hurry one, but not lead to dejection and despair.

On the contrary, help provided to others, constructive discussions with spiritual friends, progress on the Path of self-development should fill one with happiness, joy.

"Happiness is essential for God-realization. It is one of the big gateways to the Divinity. If man is unhappy, this is not just a flaw. This is one of the most serious flaws! This is an obstacle on the way to self-realization!

"In most cases people are unhappy because of worldly aspirations, attachments, and joys: they pay too much attention to the worldly.

"In order to help one to get rid of this flaw, it is necessary to point out how much serious this flaw is. One should realize that desires are never-ending like waves in a sea!" [2]

In many cases, the reason for people's suffering is that only through suffering God can convince them of the necessity of turning inside, into the *depth* of the multidimensional structure of their organisms, of the necessity of self-examination. Without this, such people will never get rid of suffering! God is inside, in the *depth*! He heals from there![5] [2]

---

[5] Going into the *depth*, however, has nothing to do with just philosophizing or even with "psychoanalytical" "picking" at one's past. *Subconsciousness* is the originally wrong term, not related in any way to the concept of *consciousness*. What is called *subconsciousness* is just that which was forgotten by the mind; it is also the manas.

"It is only when you are far from the Truth, that you suffer, feel pain, and experience travail.

"At a distance from the bazaar, one hears only a huge indistinct uproar. But, as we approach it and walk into it, one can clearly distinguish the separate bargainings.

"So too, until the reality of the Supreme is known, you are overpowered and stunned by the uproar of the world, but once you enter deep into the realm of spiritual endeavor, everything becomes clear and the knowledge of the reality awakens within you. Until then you will be caught up in the meaningless noise of argumentation, disputation and exhibitionist flamboyance.

"Everyone who seeks the Eternal through the path of bhakti (devotional love for God) should strive to acquire the following characteristics: he must keep away from the turmoils, the cruelties, and the falsehoods of this world and practice

---

The mind is meant for maintenance of life in the material world, the buddhi — in the non-material, first of all.

The manas must enter into the buddhi through submersion into the spiritual heart and there — into the depth of multidimensional organism — toward merging with the Higher Self. In that way, the personal mind of man merges with the Wisdom of God.

truth, righteousness, love, and peace. This is truly the Path of bhakti!

"Those who seek Union with God, those who seek the welfare of the world should discard as worthless both praise and blame, appreciation and derision, prosperity and adversity. No one, not even God or an Avatar can ever escape criticism and blame. But They do not yield to threats." [7]

"Man must pray for newer and newer opportunities for service and exult in the chance that his hands receive. This attitude gives immeasurable joy. To lead a life suffused with this joy is indeed bliss! ... If life is lived accordingly, then it becomes one long unbroken service to the Lord. The feeling of 'I' and 'You' will soon disappear; all traces of self will be destroyed." [7]

"Many aspirants and hermits, many sadhakas and sannyasis lost all their achievements, which they won by many years of struggle and sacrifice, because of their attachment to the self" [7].

"Whatever the wealth of words, whatever the standard of scholarship, it is all useless. In order to bring the Teachings... into the actual life, it is necessary to extirpate the feeling, 'I know,' see the very Essence and introspect on It. Only in that case one will certainly achieve bliss...

"If, however, the awareness of 'i' produces pride..., a fall is inevitable..." [7].

Service to others according to the karma yoga principles not only develops people in all criteria and makes their karma better, but also, with right attitude to this service, i.e. with experiencing oneself as an assistant of God, leads to gradual merging of one's self with the Divine Self.

"At home every member of the family does work intended for him. In the evening, when all work is done, nobody says: 'Father, I have done this work and this, you have to pay me'. This is one family, therefore you do not ask the payment for your work; you just do it.

"But if someone from the outside comes to work in your house, then you arrange about the payment and pay accordingly. What you pay to someone shows that he is not from your house.

"But when somebody becomes 'yours', it is not necessary to pay him. He works with interest, not expecting any reward for his work.

"It is the same with God. When you know that God is the closest and dearest Being for you, and that He and you are one family, you do not ask for the payment. He who devotes himself to God completely is Mine! And he should not expect any reward.

"But if somebody says: 'I have dedicated to sadhana so much time,' and establishes trade relations with God, saying at the same time: 'In my sadhana, I have done this, and I must get a reward,' then it is completely different.

"A child, who is too small, does not say to his mother: I want milk, I want my napkin changed, and so on. The mother herself keeps her eyes on what is necessary for the child without child's requests about this. When you have devoted yourself to God completely and become His child — it is not necessary to speak about what you want. He will give you even more than you would ask!

"Because of your love for Him — let Him be the dearest for you!

"Perform your sadhana, and you will approach God! When it happens, it will not be necessary for you to tell Him that you want this or that — because you will become for Him as His small child. He will come and give you even more than you ask!

"Just as a ventilator is an instrument, you are the instrument of God. Is it a ventilator which puts itself in motion? Or it is the electric current that puts it in motion?" [2].

"To entrust yourself to God means to devote to Him each thought and act not wishing (for yourself) the fruits of this act. Perform acts not because of their fruits, but because it is your duty. The act is devoted to God, and the result is reaped by Him as well.

"The acts, performed in that way, without desire for their fruits for oneself, are free from the negative karmic consequences. Because the ego during such acts is not fed and stimulated, it disappears soon." [2]

Sathya Sai Baba, as we have seen already, is against casual sexual relationships, against being obsessed with sex. But He supports marriage, family life, including upbringing of children. Marriage also helps "washing out" the primitive lower self, because the family life is favorable for transformation of the "I" into "we".

Marriage and karma yoga teach one to care for others. In that way, the ability to take care grows; this ability is an attribute of Love. In that way, the sphere of one's love extends to more and more people. One's personal "I" dissolves in the universal "we".

The further progress in that field is ensured by the meditative techniques which wash out all remaining coverings from the Higher Self.

But Sathya Sai Baba warns that one should not trust various "gurus" only on the grounds that they proclaimed themselves "guru". He says that a real guru is the one who knows God and can lead people to Him. But such people are very few. Anyway, it is much better when your guru is God.

Sathya Sai Baba also very precisely points out that meditative training is not meant for everyone. People differ between themselves by the age of souls, first of all. For young and immature souls meditative training may be destructive. Not all people can even comprehend what meditation is. For example, dreamlike mental images, such as flying to other planets, are a wrong and harmful practice [2].

The true essence of every human being is the Ocean of the Consciousness of the Creator. Our task is to develop ourselves to the stage of practical realization (not only mental understanding) of this truth through sadhana (the way of spiritual endeavor).

On this Path one should transform from a jiva (an individual soul attached to the body and material objects) to chit (the pure, i.e. a consciousness, which is cleaned and refined to the level of the Creator, and is identical to the Atman, the Higher Self of man).

A developing soul, who walks this Path, from a certain moment gains the ability to see in the subtle eons, as it explores them more and more. A human consciousness, which entered the higher eons, learns to see God — as Living Light-Fire, in particular, — and to interact with Him.

From a certain stage of buddhi yoga, adepts can experience the material world as if "superimposed" on the Light of the Divine Consciousness; then it is easy to "fall" into It, dissolve in It, become It [8].

But such a level of the meditative work is accessible only for very few successful disciples of God. For beginners, Sathya Sai Baba recommends the following series of meditative training which, for sure, cannot harm anyone [2 and others]:

Light a candle. Remember its image very well. Then transfer this image into the anahata (this can be done with one's back turned toward the candle), fill the volume of the chakra with the light, imagine in it a flower which consists of light and begins to open. Then direct the light into the arms, head, in other parts of the organism. Then fill with this light the bodies of the most beloved people, then the bodies of all people, animals, plants..., the whole world gets filled with the light; my self sinks in it and disappears; I and the light merge together; the image of the light created by me merges with the Light of the Consciousness of God...

Mastering each element of this meditation may take much time. But it is a straight path toward the cognition of God and Mergence with Him.

If one includes in this meditation a Fiery Image of Sathya Sai Baba or of any other Divine

Teacher, then such work will be much more effective.

Bhakti yoga, i.e. self-realization through love for God, is the highest yoga, the Highest, Straight Path.

The true (in potential) essence of every human being is God. God indeed resides within the multidimensional organism of man, in its very *depth*, in the subtlest eons. It is necessary just to learn to move there with the concentration of the consciousness, and then to establish oneself there. This will be the full Self-realization, God-realization of oneself, the full and final Liberation from the bondage of the world of illusions.

One achieves God-realization through love, through falling in love with God. This love allows one to sink in His Flame, in the Embrace of His Love, to merge together with the Beloved.

This is the only way of attaining the highest spiritual achievements; there are no other ways. This is what God taught during the entire history of mankind and teaches now. This is the fundamental of all serious religious systems. But people forget about this, and God has to remind them again.

One of people's problems is that they do not listen to God, but listen to various false pastors, gurus, leaders of the numerous sects. Some of them suggest themselves to people as an object of worship, instead of God. Others speak about God, yet pervert His Teachings to the opposite.

An example of it is a well-known, widely promoted sect of "yoga", where its followers — as they were — were suggested that every one of them is God, a coessential to Him Part of Universal God. They "expanded the consciousnesses" and also, as a constant practice, asked themselves: "Who am I?" The answer had to be: "Higher Self!", "God!".

The leader and the members of this sect knew neither God, nor even the direction in which one must seek Him. They recognized neither repentance, nor the necessity of the refinement of consciousness, nor love for God: Why, God is what I am!

And if I am God, then all my desires, acts are flawless, Divine! They are manifestation of the universal Divine Will!

This large sect produced a great number of primitives who considered themselves "Gods"; the primitives who lived by the coarse uncontrollable passions which became "legitimatized", "Divine" for them.

Sathya Sai Baba, answering once in a conversation, disapproved the work of this sect and said that its "guru" made spiritual progress only later on, when he stopped his activity [2].

The techniques of the *expansion of consciousness,* of its *crystallization* are very dangrous methods, in the sense that if they are given to people with non-refined consciousness or with undeveloped intellect and perverted ethics (with traits of violence, egotism), then diabolization of these people happens, in the very direct sense: they become devils. They transform to devils, dooming themselves to much suffering; they also bring to the Earth the will of the devilish eon, manifesting it trough their bodies.

Therefore, Sathya Sai Baba strongly recommends not to trust such "gurus", but to become a disciple of God. Let God be your guru! No one can put oneself between a person and God! Trust in God, and He will help you!

Love for God is the Straight Path!

From Conversations with Sathya Sai Baba

I love Sathya Sai Baba infinitely! Through this love I learned to feel myself, in meditations, a part of Him. And when He talks to me, the feeling of infinite Love-Care of my Universal Parent does not leave me.

"Baba, how can man learn to think as You think?"

"One cannot just throw away everything from the head and replace it with Me, with My Consciousness... — then one would become a biorobot, a puppet. No, one has to grow one's own intellect, one's own ability to think so. And only then — this ability to think with the consciousness[6] unites with My Divine Wisdom!

"In this way the development of soul goes on. First, man has to learn to be love and to grow as love. Then he learns to give his love for Me. In this way, gradually, he masters Mergence with Me.

"If man has no love yet... — he has no that by which he can merge with Me!

---

[6] I.e., not with the manas, but with the buddhi.

"And then love is supplemented with the aspect of power.

"When all strength of the soul you give, dedicate to serving Me[7], then you begin mastering Mergence with My Omnipotence. This is a very gradual process...

"In the same way, gradually, one can learn from Me Divine thinking.

"After all, beingness in Me means to be Me! Therefore, the flow and essence of you thoughts must correspond to this. I suggest that you master *broad thinking* — thoughts flow easily, smoothly, calmly, manifesting from the *Depth* on the physical plane. And then one can encompass with the consciousness not only forests, meadows, rivers, lakes with their inhabitants, but also countries, continents, nations and communities of people, feeling them all together and every one in particular.

"Yes, one has to learn from Me — to love, to think, to act! The lower self must be substituted with the Higher Self — your True, Divine Self, Which is coessential with the Self of God.

"... At that, this is not the end of the path. Every Soul Which became *One* with Me continues

---

[7] This constitutes the main essence of the true monasticism.

to develop in Me, growing and perfecting Its service — the service to the evolution of consciousnesses in the universe.

"Those of Us Who come incarnated to the Earth differ from each other. But not by the feature of superiority or inferiority to Others... The difference is that Some are similar to sprouts which just have appeared on the surface from the boundless *Foundation* — from the Ocean of the Creator, while Others are like strong great trees which have been growing for a long time.

"Divine *Vines* originating from Me continue Their Growth in Me and from Me — to living beings of the entire universe.

"Nevertheless, whatever great may be every One coming out from Me, He or She is but a small particle of the Great Whole Primordial *Ocean.*

"... Avatars always have something to say to people: They are direct Flows of the Divine Energy from the Creator.

"I am going to tell you about how live Those Who became *One* with the Father. They live helping people to cognize their Higher Nature. They live manifesting the Father. And Everyone learns to help...

"I learn too...

"Shirdi Sai Baba was a Saint only to the small number of people who were near His body.

"Sathya Sai Baba became close to millions of people on the Earth. Many of them have never seen My body; nevertheless, I became a reality of their lives.

"When I was a boy Narayana, I talked only to those who saw the eyes of My body. And now I really help many of My followers living in bodies of children, adults, and old men. The love of Sathya Sai Baba for them — and their love for Sathya Sai Baba — in an instant! — connects Me with everyone like a current: man pushes a button to light up the bulb of love — and My Current flows to him!

"I do this in all corners of the Earth; the distance does not matter here. I come to them so that they can hear My voice, see Me. When they urgently need My help, I react instantly and redirect there a part of My Power. And miracles happen there. This is the reality of relationships of man with God.

"I learned to do this. It is not the body of Sathya Sai Baba that does this, but a Part of Me as a Consciousness, which is present in the Creation and works there; this Part is giant.

"I also heal the bodies of My followers by guiding the hands of surgeons during operations. I write books with those who do this for

Me. And I just sing bhajans[8] with those who cannot do anything else yet.

"... I easily manifest Myself on different levels of the density of consciousness.

"Look: now I am of a human body in height..." Baba shows Himself walking slowly over the road in the park where our conversation is taking place: He walks as He does on darshan: orange robe, thick dark hair, it seems that I can touch them with my hands.

"Or I can enter your body..." and Sathya Sai Baba looks through the eyes of my body at the leaves falling slowly from trees; then He moves my arms...

Then He showed His Face familiar to us from communication with Him. His Face is a half of the trees' height in size... It is made of Light-Love, Light-Tenderness; and His Arms can take on the Palms any soul on the planet and know about it everything...

"And this is Me — Universal!..." Sathya Sai Baba appears in a Giant Mahadouble coming out from the Ocean of the Primordial Consciousness.

"The Brahmanic part of Me is so great that I can be everywhere — whenever it is necessary.

---

[8] Songs which praise God and accustom one to love for Him.

"It is very important to learn to live being a consciousness free from the body: to love, to hear, to perceive, to speak, to act!

"To be and to act from the Ocean of God-the-Father here, in the world of matter, is possible only out of the Great Love for *His children*. This is the state in which God comes to this world!

"Also to be able to awake the hearts of people one must have also... the Divine patience!"

"Tell us please about the Divine patience. How can one gain it?"

"*Patience* is the foundation of *calm*, the basis of the true ability of working creatively. The more *patience* man has the higher he can achieve in all areas of life, and, of course, — in cognition of Me.

"*Patience* must not be passive: what use is to be patient doing nothing? No, the true *patience* is an active state.

"One must patiently, step by step, reform in oneself all defects of the soul, reform oneself in accordance with the *ethics of God*. In the process of such work, one gains the Divine Patience.

"*Patience* also necessary for understanding of other people. One has to learn to understand other people! Without such understanding one cannot help them!

"I understand everyone who addresses Me. And My understanding results in people's trusting

Me. Trust is the foundation of faith. The true faith manifests itself as full *trust in Me*.

"*Trust in Me* is born and grows when man addresses Me, not only in the moments of despair, but always: in sorrow and in joy, in work and in rest, being sick and being healthy. In the process of constant communication and interaction of the soul with Me, mutual understanding and trust are born, the true faith is formed, which is founded on one's own experience and knowledge.

"Everyone can fill their life with Me to a certain degree. This is very simple: one has to open the heart and invite Me into it! Also one has to learn to ask Me questions. God also has a *Divine Etiquette*: I never come there where I was not invited, I do not answer unasked questions. Observing the *Law of freedom of will*, I do not interfere with people's lives without necessity.

"... Love is multifaceted... You can know its various aspects: love-friendship, love-care, love-tenderness, love-respect and reverence...

"And now — unite all this together!

"And let friendship be without dependence, care — without attachments, tenderness — without the desire to possess...

"To love means to give, to shine with the Light of Love, to be Love in all Its fullness, purity, and transparency!

"Also — watch Me, watch My every move, My every thought. I guide every one of you! In particular — through deeds of vile people...

"Also remember that I derail those trains which travel unloaded...

"Ponder: what is your goal? The answer is simple and obvious: to become Me completely!

"To become Me, to be Me — what can be higher than this? It is in My Beingness that you will find all the Highest that man can dream of!

"Explain this to people! Unfold to them this Goal in all its majestic greatness! Let everyone understand that God is not a ruler-usurper, but that in Him is the highest Freedom of everyone, the Freedom which most people cannot even conceive now!

"... First, a seeker, who dedicated his life to Me, has to come to know what it is like — to be Me.

"Then he has to make a decision to sacrifice the life which he lived before — for the sake of coming to My Life in its fullness. And such a sincere seeker receives My help.

"Gradually, he must abandon his old way of life and transform his life to that Life which I open for him.

"When in his life there remains nothing of the cravings of the lower self and there is only Me — then he becomes truly a Part of Me.

"God cannot give Himself to those who do not yearn for Him with all the heart!

"All who seek to cognize Me have to kindle in themselves a great yearning for Me — for the Ocean of My Love! I want from people not a languid remembering about God...

"Everyone striving for the full cognition of God has to make Me — their main Goal! Meditation brings true fruits only when love flares up so that between you and Me no obstacles remain! And then — your separateness does not exist any longer!

"The true cognition of God begins only when the flame of your heart becomes a part of the *Divine Fire*. Only when you become the *Fire of Love* — you may know the main Essence of yourself, Which is God in the aspect of the Creator!"

"How can one kindle such love in people more successfully?"

"Fire is kindled by fire...

"My burning Love touches the hearts of incarnate people and ignites the souls!

"One has to bring people to the threshold where they come in touch with Me. And then let every one remain there one-to-one with Me.

"If a soul, after touching Me, continues to shine for others — then this is the true burning!"

"You told us that You are going to leave the body, to leave the earthly plane. And what about the millions of Your followers — how will You build Your relationships with them?"

"I will remain with everyone who entrusted themselves to Me. I will continue to guide them through their lives to My Abode — to the Primordial Ocean of the Universal Consciousness. I will talk to them through you too. Many times I tried the purity of your hearts, the strength of your love, thereliability of your hands. And now I know: your hands are My Hands, your hearts are My Heart! I bless you to continue My work on the Earth!

"Fill souls with My Light so that they may arise to life in Love!

"I radiate the Brahmanic Light through your Atmic Mahadoubles; They are like Light pipes...

"The strata of the Absolute are your 'clothes' and you live beneath them.

"Always perceive your new Atmic Bodies[9] — *to the Full Height!* You have to learn to live with them; in this process the physical body becomes

---

[9] Atmans in Paramatman.

divine and the soul's controlling center moves into Paramatman — into the 'I' of God!

"The total freedom from the body is possible when it is separated from the consciousness through death. Yet, another freedom is also possible — as much total as the first one! — without the death of the body. It requires treatment of the body with the Consciousness of the Creator...

"The meditative principle 'there is no "me"[10] in the body' means: 'I am!' I am as the Higher Self!' This constitutes the full transfer of the self-awareness in My Abode and conscious actions from it.

"People Who have learned to be the *Ocean* — They live connected with the Infinity of Me...

"... And do not think about money which you 'cannot get from anywhere'!

"Jesus had nothing on the Earth and did not always know what He would eat and where He would sleep with His disciples. Yet, this did not prevent Him from carrying out His Mission...

"And Krishna, after the battle, did not possess any earthly wealth: they left carrying nothing; their only wealth was the memories which they

---

[10] Lower self.

44

left to the future generations... At the moment of the death of His body, Krishna was as rich as Jesus dying on the cross: They were richer than other people, for They not just gave Themselves to Me, but changed the history of the Earth by Their Lives — and even today souls *flow into Me through Their Channels*!

"Now it is your turn!...

"Let all your dreams and intentions become Mine!

"Let all your aspirations become Mine!

"Let all your decisions become Mine!

"Let all your love become My Love!

"Let all your deeds become My Deeds!

"Let all your desires become My Desires!

"Let all your life become My Life!"

Bibliography

1. Maheshwarand — Sai Baba and the Nara Narayana Gufa Ashram. "Society for Vedic Culture", Saint Petersburg, 1993 *(in Russian)*.

2. Hislop J. — Conversations with Bhagavan Sri Sathya Sai Baba. "Society for Vedic Culture", Saint Petersburg, 1994 *(in Russian)*.

3. Hislop J. — My Baba and I. "Sri Sathya Sai Books and Publications Trust", Prasanthi Nilayam, 1985.

4. Sandweiss S. — Sathya Sai — The Holy Man and... the Psychiatrist. "Society for Vedic Culture", Saint Petersburg, 1991 *(in Russian)*.

5. Sathya Sai Baba — Selected Discourses and Articles by Sathya Sai Baba from the Journal Sanathana Sarathi, Saint Petersburg, 1995 *(in Russian)*.

6. Sathya Sai Baba — Sayings. "Center 'Sathya'", Saint Petersburg, 1991 *(in Russian)*.

7. Sathya Sai Baba — Prema Vahini. The Stream of Divine Love. "Society for Vedic Culture", Saint Petersburg, 1993 *(in Russian)*.

8. Sathya Sai Baba — Sandeha Nivarini. Clearance of Spiritual Doubts. "Society for Vedic Culture", Saint Petersburg, 1993 *(in Russian)*.

9. Sathya Sai Baba — Prasnottara Vahini. Answers to Spiritual Questions. "Society for Vedic Culture", Saint Petersburg, 1993 *(in Russian)*.

10. Sathya Sai Baba — Jnana Vahini. The Stream of Eternal Wisdom. "Society for Vedic Culture", Saint Petersburg, 1997 *(in Russian)*.

11. Sathya Sai Baba — Yoga of Action. Significance of Selfless Service. "Center of Sathya Sai", Saint Petersburg, 1997 *(in Russian)*.

12. Sudha Aditya — Nectarine Showers of Sathya Sai. Saint Petersburg, 1996 *(in Russian)*.

1630057